Contents

All England Netball Association Limited
Netball House
9 Paynes Park
Hitchin
Hertfordshire
SG5 1EH

tel 01462 442344

Acknow...
Text by Mary Thomas.
The publishers would like to thank Mitre
Sports for their photographic contribution
to this book.

mitre®

Photographs on the front cover, the inside
front cover, pages 3, 14 (centre), 18, 36,
the inside back cover and the back cover
courtesy of Eileen Langsley.
Photographs on pages 9, 15 (top right)
and 34 (right) courtesy of Brian Worrell.
Photographs on pages 29 and 30 courtesy
of William Hickey.
Illustrations by Tim Bairstow of Taurus
Graphics.

Note Throughout the book players
and officials are referred to individually
as 'she'. This should, of course, be taken
to mean 'she or he', since netball is now
played by both sexes.

Introduction

Netball is an international sport traditionally played by women, although the rules allow for male participation as long as any one game is single sex.

The game is played on a comparatively small hard court area between two teams of seven players. For beginners and young players netball's simple organisation and equipment make the game easily understood. However, restrictions in playing area, the rule controlling footwork, and the non-contact nature of the sport all challenge high-level precision skills. Netball has the merit of wide appeal, offering enjoyable recreation to most participants, but also attracting highly talented athletes at the top.

In setting out this book, all the essential rules of netball are included, but not necessarily in the order of the Official Rules book.

Young players enjoying themselves ▶

Conditions for play

The court (Rule 1.1)

The court surface must be firm to allow for the precise and controlled footwork which characterises netball skill. A loose top surface could be dangerous. A soft or soggy surface does not suit the game's skills and, since players may not wear shoes with spiked soles, the surface must be non-slip.

Fig. 1 below shows the measurements which are required for the court on which netball is played, and names the lines and areas. Lines are part of the court and must not be more than 50 mm (2 in) wide. From within the court, whenever a player's foot is *on* a line she is still in her legal playing area (*Rule 8*).

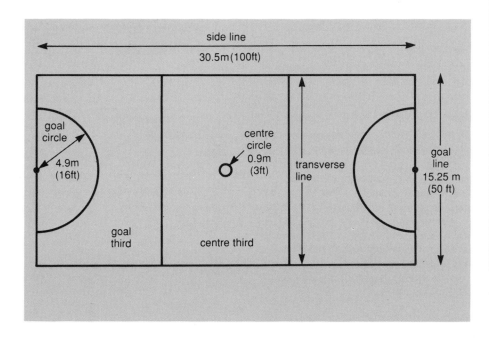

side line

30.5m (100ft)

goal circle

4.9m (16ft)

centre circle 0.9m (3ft)

transverse line

goal line

15.25 m (50 ft)

goal third

centre third

◀ *Fig. 1 The court*

The goalpost (Rule 1.2)

A goal is scored when either a goal shooter or a goal attack in one team is standing wholly within the goal circle and throws or bats the ball over and completely through the ring attached to the goalpost (*Rule 15*).

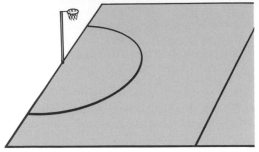

Fig. 2 Location of the goalpost ▲ ▶

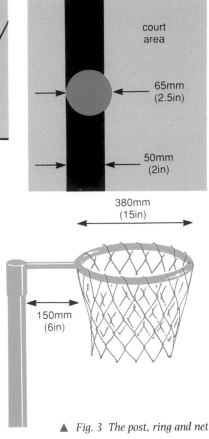

The goalpost is a vertical pole either inserted into a socket in the ground or supported by a metal base. It must be 3.05 m (10 ft) high and may be round, with a diameter measuring anything between 65 mm (2.5 in) to 100 mm (4 in) or the same measurements square. The goalpost is placed in the centre of the goal line so that the back of the post is at the outside of the line.

The ring through which a goal is scored projects horizontally 150 mm (6 in) from the top of the post. The steel rod ring must have an internal diameter of 380 mm (15 in) and be fitted with a net open at both ends.

Both ring and net are considered to be part of the goalpost.

▲ *Goalpost, with shooters in action*

▲ *Fig. 3 The post, ring and net*

The ball *(Rule 1.3)*

The ball, made from leather, rubber or similar material, may be bought as a netball or a size 5 football (they are the same). When inflated, the ball should measure between 690 mm (27 in) and 710 mm (28 in) in circumference and weigh between 400 g (14 oz) and 450 g (16 oz). An easy test for the right 'feel' is to apply pressure with the fingers to the surface of the ball and to check that there is very little indentation. Young players may benefit from learning to play with a size 4 ball until their hands have grown enough to spread over the surface of the larger ball.

▲ *A netball*

A complete team ▶

The players
(Rules 1.4, 4 and 8)

Seven players on court at any one time make a team *(Rule 4)*. The game is designed for single sex competition, and the playing positions are: Goal Shooter (GS), Goal Attack (GA), Wing Attack (WA), Centre (C), Wing Defence (WD), Goal Defence (GD) and Goal Keeper (GK).

Substitutions are allowed during play *(see* page 47), although a game may be played if only five or six players from a team are on court.

Each player is allowed in only a limited area of the court. While in this area, the player is onside. If she goes into the wrong area she is offside. Together, the playing position and the playing area tell a player what contribution she makes to teamwork. All players need similar basic skills, but their playing positions emphasise some of these skills more than others.

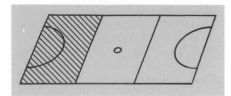

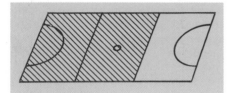

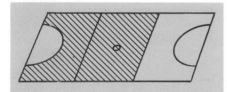

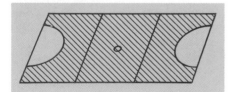

Playing areas

GS: her main job is to score goals. She uses less energy than some players, because she has a small area in which to move. This helps her to retain the stamina to concentrate on shooting.

GA: her job is twofold: to score goals, and to contribute to the attacking play in the goal third in order to move the ball towards the circle. Occasionally, she will contribute to the attack in the centre third.

WA: her main job is to receive the ball in the attacking goal third in the best position from which to pass the ball into the circle. She will be ready to help in the centre third, but is expected to have the energy to dodge about many times in the goal third while working for that good position to pass into the circle.

C: she has to contribute to the attack and defence in all areas of the court except the circles. She needs the most stamina but also good observation, because she has to make decisions about when to move to receive the ball

▲ *A Centre involved in play*

▼ *A Centre observing proceedings*

and when to move out of the way to create space for someone in her team who is in a better position.

WD: her critical work is to defend the opposing WA. Because a good WA will have concentrated on mastering a variety of dodging moves and excellent passing to precise places, the WD must mark to block the WA's movement and defend the ball to upset the passing.

GD: her job is very similar to that of the WD, although she has the added area of the goal circle to cover. Because her opponent, the GA, will always want to make her final movement towards the goal, the GD must learn to read her opponent's intention in order to block the move. She needs the specialist skill of defending a shot for goal.

GK: she has to defend – and defend again and again – aiming to prevent her opponent receiving the ball; to defend the shot at goal as a second line of defence; to retrieve a missed shot under the post as the third line of defence; and to make a perfect pass out of the circle if she gets the ball.

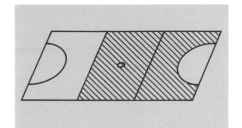

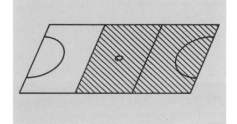

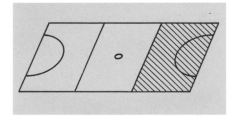

Close contest: GK intercepting ▶

Experience, coaching and planning will alter the patterns of teamwork for attack and defence as teams seek to outwit opponents, but such tactics cannot change the main emphasis of a player's job. This emphasis is dictated by the rule concerning playing positions (*Rule 8*).

Clothing *(Rule 1.4)*

The initials of playing positions must be worn by players on both the front and back above the waist, and the letters must be 160 mm (6 in) high. Registered uniforms are required by rule, though it is clearly to the team's advantage to be able to see each other quickly during the stress of competition. Shoes are the most important single item of clothing and as long as they are of light-weight material and do not have spiked soles, players should choose whatever gives them a feeling of comfort, support and durability.

A team's uniform can be fun, even fashionable, but needs to retain the essentials of ease of movement, absorbency and appropriate warmth. Jewellery is not allowed (although a wedding ring may be taped). This is to prevent possible injury to oneself or to other players. For the same reason, finger-nails must be cut short.

Duration of a game *(Rule 2)*

A match is of one hour's duration, organised into four quarters of 15 minutes each. Between the first and second, and third and fourth quarters an interval of 3 minutes is taken, while the half-time interval is 5 minutes. Before the start of the game, the captains toss to determine which one will have the choice of the first centre pass or the goal end into which they will shoot (*Rule 3.4*). After each quarter, the teams change the ends into which they are shooting.

There is provision for altering the length of a game as participants wish. The rule acknowledges that in certain

▼ *Light-weight shoes*

climates, or when teams play more than one match in a day, it may be necessary or wise to change the time. In these cases two halves of 20 minutes with a 5-minute interval at half-time is suggested, though teams may agree an alternative. Where one-day tournaments or games between young players are played, there can be even more variation in time. Games may vary from as little as 7 minutes for each half to as much as 15 minutes, or be organised into four quarters of 9, 10 or even 12 minutes each.

Organising a game

The aim of the game is to score goals after working the ball towards one's own goal in a manner allowed by the rules. The patterns of play come about by wise exploitation of the rule governing playing areas, so players must keep onside and know what happens if they go offside (*Rule 9*) or the ball goes out of court (*Rule 10*). Before such patterns can develop, it is necessary to know how to start the game (*Rules 11 and 12*) and then what rule governs goal scoring (*Rule 15*), in addition to what has already been established by *Rules 4 and 8*.

▼ *WA receiving a centre pass*

Start of play (*Rules 11 and 12*)

Centre passes

Before the start of play, only the two centres may be in the centre third. All other players may be in any part of their own goal third. The game starts with a

centre pass taken by the centre of the team in possession of the ball. This centre must be standing inside the centre circle, though one foot may be off the ground. The other centre may be standing or moving anywhere inside the centre third as long as she is not obstructing.

After the umpire blows the whistle for the centre pass, the ball must be caught within the centre third by any one of the four players in fig.4, although if a defending player intercepts this pass, play continues. These players can start from any point along the transverse line or within their goal third and may move in any direction to land at any point within the centre third.

Fig. 4 Centre passes ▶

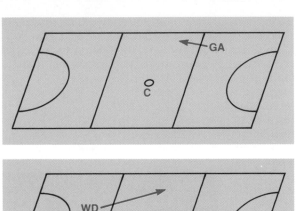

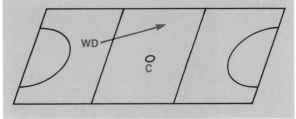

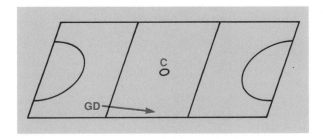

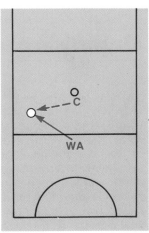

A pattern of passing develops from that point to get the ball to one of the shooters in the circle; very many different patterns will be used during the game. Two are illustrated in fig. 5, showing the pathway of the ball to the receiving players. While the ball travels in these patterns, the players are running, dodging and re-positioning to be ready to receive a pass at all times.

As soon as the GS or the GA has the ball in the goal circle she is allowed to shoot (take a shot for goal) or pass the ball again if she is not in a good position to shoot. If a shot is successful, the game returns to the line-up for the start of play. A centre pass, which is taken alternately by the two centres, re-starts the game.

More details from
Rules 11 and 12

● At the start of play, players may not move into the centre third before the whistle is blown. Because umpires should check that players are in their correct areas before blowing the whistle, players are seldom penalised for this fault unless they persist in running

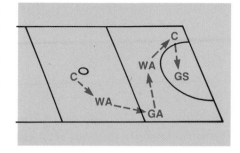

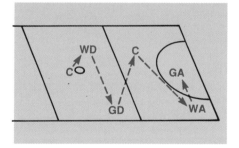

◄ *Fig. 5 Patterns of passing*

over the line while the umpire is checking. If two players simultaneously break this rule, the umpire does nothing unless either touches the ball, in which case a toss-up is taken.
● When the whistle is blown, the centre with the ball must release it within 3

seconds and must obey the footwork rule. If the ball is still in the centre's hands when time is signalled for the end of a quarter, the same centre takes the centre pass when play re-starts.
● When receiving a centre pass, it is permitted for a player to land with one foot only just inside the centre third as long as it is the *first* landing foot. Landing first on one foot in the goal third is not permitted even if the second foot subsequently lands in the centre third. Neither is a simultaneous landing on feet astride the transverse line permitted. 'Receiving' the centre pass means either catching the ball or touching it.

The landing point is not important if a defending player is the first to touch or catch the centre pass; play continues.

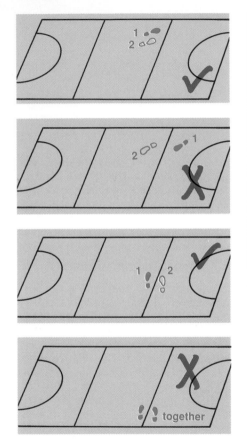

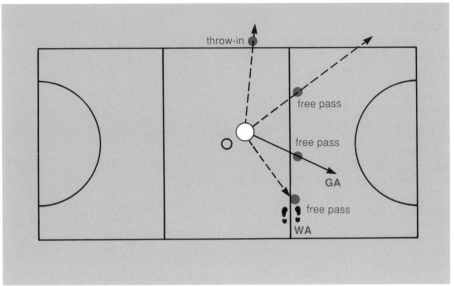

● A free pass is awarded for any fault in receiving the ball except that a throw-in is awarded if the ball goes out of court over the side line bounding the centre third.

▲ *Fig. 7 Centre pass: a free pass is awarded for any fault in receiving the ball, except when the ball goes out of court over the side line bounding the centre third, when a throw-in is awarded*

◄ *Fig. 6 After receiving the centre pass, this WA has four landing possibilities*

Scoring a goal *(Rule 15)*

Shooters must learn some details which the rule sets out in order to discipline play in the circle:

● shooters must be wholly within the circle to shoot and may make no contact with the ground outside the circle either during the catching of the ball or while holding it. If they are *on* the line, or if they lean on the ball which is on the ground in the court area outside the circle, they may recover and shoot
● shooters may retrieve their own missed shot and shoot again, as long as the ball touches any part of the goalpost, including the net. They may retrieve the other shooter's missed shot and shoot immediately
● shooters are bound by all other rules which discipline skilled play, including Footwork, Playing the ball, Obstruction and Contact.

Shooters need to know all other parts of the rule to promote their own quick response to play in the goal circle:

● if either shooter is involved in a toss-up in the circle, she may choose to shoot or pass if she wins the ball
● if a free pass is taken by a shooter standing within the circle, a pass and not a shot for goal must be made
● if a penalty pass or shot is awarded to the shooting team within the circle, either player may take the ball and choose whether to shoot or to pass
● if a shot at goal is disrupted because a defending player moves the goalpost, a penalty pass or shot will be awarded to the shooting team
● if a ball goes through the ring from a shooter's shot for goal, even though a defending player touched the ball in flight, the goal is scored
● if the whistle for 'time' is blown just after a penalty pass or shot is awarded, the shot shall be taken
● if the ball travels over and through the ring from a pass by any other player from any other position, no goal is scored. Play continues from where the ball is caught and shooters who know the rule well can move quickly to retrieve the disallowed 'shot'. There will be no umpire's whistle to guide them

● when the whistle is blown for 'time' after a shot has been made, a goal is scored only if the ball has passed completely through the ring, though not necessarily out of the net
● when the ball is out of court and a throw-in is awarded to the attacking team, either shooter must take the throw-in if it is awarded at any point behind the line bounding the goal circle, though any player allowed in that area may take the throw-in at other places along the goal line.

Techniques to help the shooting action

It is necessary to *lift* the ball high to reach the height of the ring. The photographs on the next page show parts of the sequence, from the slightly downward preparation to the upward extension which will push the ball high. This movement will increase in speed to the point of release, though too much speed will cause the ball to travel over the ring without scoring.

▲ *Shooter prepares down*

central picture showing the shooter having taken the ball above the defender's hand.

The forward movement which finally completes the shot will be made almost exclusively by the wrist through to the fingers in shots taken near the post, and from the elbow through the forearm first when more power is required.

In all the photographs, notice: the position of the feet; the fingers – whether holding, supporting or pushing the ball; the vertical body positions; and the focus of the shooters' eyes which look just above and to the back of the ring and not at the defender's hand.

It is necessary to lift high *before* making any forward movement, because a good defending opponent will have limited the space within which the shooter's arm can move without causing contact with the ball (*Rule 17.2.1*). The photographs on page 15 show the limited space, the

▼ *Shooter now half up*

▼ *Shooter completely up*

▲ Stepping away from the defence for a shot

▼ Another backward step

▲ Shooter has limited space because of the defender's hand position

▲ Shooter takes the ball above the defender's hand

Shooters who are being worried by a good defender's long reach and forward lean may sometimes step sideways or backwards before shooting. It is still possible to retain all the wise techniques which help shooting, though balance is more difficult and it is even more important to emphasise the vertical body position and arm movement before the release of the ball.

Rules governing start of play and scoring a goal presuppose a knowledge of the earlier rules about playing areas and playing positions. Playing a game disciplined by these regulations requires an understanding of two other rules, Offside and Out of court.

Offside (Rule 9)

Players must keep within their own playing area and are offside if they go elsewhere. A player offside is penalised.

Umpires are not required to note and evaluate whether the offside player: is holding or has touched the ball; has gone offside deliberately or accidentally; has wholly entered the offside area or has only a small part of one foot offside; or enters momentarily or remains off-

side. All these situations describe offside faults. The opposing team is given a free pass at that point in the offside area where the defaulting player first crossed the boundary line. Even when taking a throw-in a player may be judged offside, for she must take it only from behind her own playing area.

When *two* players go offside simultaneously there are judgements to make:

- if neither player catches or touches the ball, there is no penalty and play continues
- if either one catches or touches the

ball, a toss-up is taken between them in their own onside area
- if both catch or touch the ball, a toss-up is taken in the same way.

Usually, these offside occasions occur when two opposing players are near each other, both working to get free or defend in order to get the ball.

Occasionally, the two players may not be close (*see* fig. 8), but may still simultaneously be offside. A toss-up in their area at a point mid-way between them should then be taken.

Even more occasionally, the two

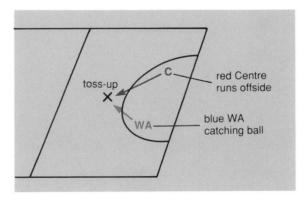

◀ *Fig. 8 Simultaneous offside*

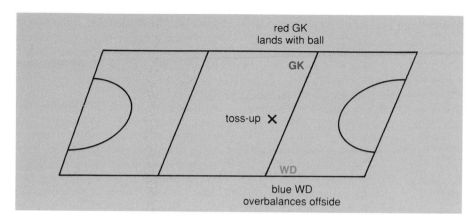

red GK
lands with ball

GK

toss-up ✕

WD

blue WD
overbalances offside

▲ *Fig.9 Two offside players with no common playing area*

offside players do not have a common playing area (*see* fig. 9). As one has the ball, the penalty is awarded, but in this case is taken between any two opposing players allowed in the centre third where the toss-up should be taken.

The *ball* cannot be offside, so if a player reaches from her onside area to pick up or lean on the ball which is in her offside area, there is no fault as long as she does not touch the ground.

Out of court (*Rule 10*)

A summary of the many clauses contained in this rule could be:

the ball *cannot go out of court but a* player *can, although there are conditions governing defending actions for out-of-court players and the re-entry of players who have left the court.*

Details which account for this summary are as follows.

The ball is out if it touches the ground, touches any object such as a wall, tree or person who is in contact with the ground, or is in the hands of a player touching the ground out of court.

The repetition of 'the ground' is important because air space beyond the court area is not regarded as out of court. A player can be standing on court and leaning sideways to retrieve a ball in the air above the ground out of court. She can jump from inside the court and bat a ball which is in the air outside the court area and, if it arrives back on the court, play will continue even if she lands outside.

A player is only judged to be out of court if she is in possession of the ball and one of the conditions for the ball being out of court applies. A player can stand or move out for tactical reasons though she must re-enter the court before attempting to play the ball. The defending players must be within the court in order to take any defending action.

If a player has to leave the court to retrieve a ball or take a throw-in, she must be allowed back on to the court near to that spot as long as she does not choose to stay out for tactical reasons.

The penalty for all out of court decisions is a throw-in to the opposing team where the ball left the court.

The penalty for a defending player's illegal attempt to prevent someone from re-entering the court is a penalty pass or shot on court where the defending player was standing.

If two opposing players jump and catch a ball simultaneously, but one lands out of court, a toss-up is taken on court between those two players.

A player is not out of court if she is *on* the line and, because the goalpost is on the line, a ball which strikes the post is not out of court if it rebounds on to the court area.

Controlling skill – I

Apart from shooting, the primary skills of netball are throwing and catching. They must be wisely controlled by good technique and legally controlled by the requirements of *Rule 13*, Playing the ball. Both the technique and the discipline are bound further by *Rule 14*, Footwork. Together, these two rules account for netball's characteristic style of play, just as the organisation of playing positions and areas of play account for the tactical style of the game. The interaction between skill and rule is explained first.

Catching

A player *may* (*Rule 13*) catch the ball with one or both hands and, prior to catching it, may bat or bounce the ball once, or tip the ball in an uncontrolled manner once or more than once. This last action is most likely to occur during a contest with an opponent when both are striving to reach a ball in the air.

Having caught or held the ball, a player *may not* drop the ball and replay it. 'Replay' means the player may neither catch the ball again, nor bat/bounce it for someone else in her team to catch or retrieve.

A player *may* (*Rule 14*) receive the ball while one or both feet are grounded or jump to catch and land on one or both feet. Thereafter, the rule sets limitations on the amount of travel allowed after the landing which can be summarised as: 'only one more complete step is allowed, though the landing foot may be lifted before throwing the ball'.

These excerpts from *Rules 13 and 14* illustrate why catching *must* be very controlled. Unsafe hands will cause fumbling, resulting in 'bouncing/batting more than once' or 'replaying the ball' which are not allowed. Poor timing in preparation for the catch is likely to lead to a player losing her balance. Poor anticipation during the catch will also leave a player unready to control the landing within the limitations set by the rule.

The players in the following photographs show some aspects of good catching technique which include:

- anticipating the catch: stretch or jump to reach the ball early
- covering a large surface of the ball: spread and curve the fingers

▼ *Stretch or jump to reach the ball early*

- absorbing the speed of the ball: 'give' by bending the arms
- anticipating the landing: if this is with one foot, thrust it towards the ground but prepare to bend on contact. The second foot can be used to complete the balance or to assist a body swerve into the direction of the throw. A two-footed landing is only wise if a player is well balanced in the air.

Action for one-handed catching is identical, though it is wise to complete the action by bringing the other hand on to the ball for extra security.

▲ *Body swerve*

▲ *One-handed catch*

Other actions allowed or restricted by *Rule 13*

While preparing to catch, a player *may*:

● gain control of the ball if it rebounds from any part of the goalpost, including the net. Normally this rule affects only a shooter or defence trying to gain or regain possession of the ball after a missed shot. Occasionally a badly thrown ball will hit the post and rebound on to court
● reach towards a ball on the ground and roll it towards herself in order to pick it up.

While preparing to catch, a player *may not*:

● attempt to gain possession of the ball while lying, sitting or kneeling on the ground, or by deliberately falling on to the ball
● step outside the court and then jump from this position to catch the ball and land inside the court (this would be an out-of-court infringement)
● hold on to the goalpost for support while reaching for a ball.

Once in possession of the ball, a player *may*:

● as a result of insecure balance, lean on the ball on the ground as long as it is on the court and even if it is in an offside area.

Once in possession of the ball, a player *may not*:

● keep possession for more than 3 seconds
● lean on the goalpost
● throw the ball while lying, sitting or kneeling on the ground. If a player falls, she must regain her footing and throw within 3 seconds of first catching the ball
● roll the ball to another player
● release the ball, either accidentally or deliberately, and replay it; this includes the drop mentioned earlier, and a toss, a bounce, or a throw if the ball is then replayed by the original player. It also applies to a missed shot which has not touched the goalpost.

At no time is a player allowed to strike the ball with a fist, deliberately kick the ball (if a ball hits the leg accidentally and rebounds, it is not a kick), or use the goalpost for any action other than shooting.

Throwing and footwork (*Rule 14*)

The Footwork rule, more than any other single rule, gives netball a distinctive character. It sets out the requirements for a remarkable degree of control considering the speed of running, turning and movement into jumping which good netball players achieve. A summary of its restrictions has been introduced in the context of skilled catching. A more positive approach to its details can be taken when footwork as an element in throwing skill is considered.

After completing a catch with just one foot on the ground, a player *may* step with the other foot in any direction, lift the landing foot and throw or shoot before this foot is regrounded (*Rule 14*).

To achieve throwing power, whether for speed or to cover distance, a player should start with more weight on the back foot and take a driving step forward on to the front foot, transferring weight in conjunction with the forward thrust of the arm. Lifting the landing foot may occur naturally as a result of the forward momentum, but care must be taken not to drag this foot. A player should be penalised for dragging or sliding the landing foot.

Compare these two descriptions and notice that the legal movement (rule) and wise movement (skill) require similar feet actions. The difference is that the description for the throw, including 'driving step' and 'thrust' of the arm, suggests the addition of speed and size.

Other relationships between rule and skill are now set out. For simplicity, the landing throughout is assumed to be on *one* foot and the description is of movement allowed after the landing. The right foot is chosen because, for a right-handed player, a right followed by a left foot landing is a better base for efficient throwing. If the landing is on the left foot, the same rule requirements apply. If the landing is on two feet, a player may choose which foot to move. As soon as one is lifted the other is treated like the landing foot and subsequent movement is identical.

- *A player may ... step with the other foot in any direction any number of times, pivoting on the landing foot. The pivoting foot may be lifted, but the player must throw or shoot before regrounding it.*

Footwork skill

To achieve balance, less skilled players will step on to the other foot almost immediately. If they are still not balanced, they should keep the right foot firmly on the ground and take more small steps 'any number of times' until they are steady. If they are not facing in the direction for the throw, the right foot still stays down to act as the pivot, while the left takes more steps to turn the player, or to achieve a more efficient stride length.

Throwing skill

A player should be prepared to adjust the direction of a throw to pass it to the space where the receiver hopes to catch it. Pivoting contributes to this skill. Skilled players will retain their balance on both feet until required to pass in response to the signals of other players. Their final step with the left foot pointing towards where the ball is to arrive is one factor which controls accuracy in passing.

- *A player may ... jump from the landing foot on to the other foot and jump again, but must throw the ball or shoot before regrounding either foot.*

It requires great skill from a player who is airborne to recognise from the positioning and movement of other players that she can land, gain ground and throw without any pause in her movement. The decision to take such action is exceptionally fast, resulting in the right foot landing being used as a springboard for an immediate jump on to the left foot which is itself a springboard for a jump while throwing. Synchronised with the footwork, the arms are preparing for the appropriate throw. The actual jumps may be dramatically high, but it is more usual for the first to be a 'bound', which is rather like a very springy running step. Another version of this footwork is often used when players are taking a free pass or a penalty shot. They stand on the spot indicated, then deliberately jump for-wards before throwing or shooting, in order to be nearer the receiver or the goalpost.

- *A player may ... step with the other foot and jump, but must throw the ball ...*

Here, the step is likely to be just a preparation into the jump, because a thrower wants to rise above a defending player. The throw requires very fast arm movements, since the preparation and movement into release of the ball must be achieved while the player is still air-borne. A good training practice for this skill is to have players standing on a bench, or something of similar height, in possession of the ball: they jump off the bench and pass the ball accurately to a moving player before landing on the ground.

Some other facts

- While in possession of the ball, players *may not* jump from one foot and land on the same foot (hop); nor may they jump from two feet and land back on two, although they may land on one.
- For any faults of footwork observed by the umpire, a free pass should be awarded to the opposing team from that point where the incorrect step or jump landed or where a slide started.
- When the free pass, or indeed any other penalty, is taken, the player is expected to obey the footwork rule as if the foot grounded at the point indicated by the umpire is equivalent to a one-footed landing. A player arriving at the spot before being given the ball should be treated as if she received the ball with both feet grounded.
- A player required to respond to an umpire's signal to re-start play is not observed for foot faults until after the signal is given, i.e. the centre at a centre pass; a player taking a throw-in; the player with the ball re-starting after a stoppage.

Throwing and playing the ball *(Rule 13)*

After catching the ball a player may:

- throw it in any manner and in any direction to another player
- bounce it with one or both hands in any direction to another player. Before catching the ball a player may 'pass it' (or 'direct it') by batting or bouncing it towards another player. This action could be deliberate or accidental. After contacting a ball by using one bounce or bat, or by tipping it in an uncontrol-led manner, a player may 'pass' (or 'direct') it to another player by batting or bouncing it as before.

These excerpts from *Rule 13* suggest that throwing is limited by few restrictions of rule. Knowing how best to throw is largely concerned with techni-cal matters. Just two other rules con-cern distances within which throws may be made. A ball may not be thrown over a whole third of the court, crossing two transverse lines. Therefore, the maximum distance required for a pass during play is likely to be no more than the one illustrated in fig. 10.

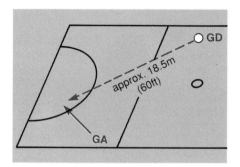

▲ *Fig. 10 A ball may not be thrown over a whole third of the court, crossing two transverse lines. This throw is legitimate*

This player (*right*) shows a technique which makes such a pass possible. Her feet are placed in such a way as to allow for the transference of weight discussed earlier under Footwork. Her arm is well drawn back, giving space for a long pull forwards while gathering speed to produce power, and this movement will include the rotation to bring the right

shoulder forwards. A final accelerating flick from the wrist as if her fingers are trying to push through the ball adds power, while the inevitable follow-through will be exaggerated to discipline the direction of the pass. To prepare, she would have made a rapid backward movement to make the ball 'stick' to her hand.

In contrast, a short pass is defined by *Rule 13* as follows: 'at the moment the ball is passed there must be room for a third player to move between the hands of the thrower and those of the receiver'.

This definition is somewhat imprecise, requiring judgement of what is 'room to move' and a strict observation of where hands are in space. The reason for allowing some space is to allow defenders to attempt interceptions without making contact. However, the rule does mean that players can be very close when passing, requiring both precision and delicacy. Wrist and finger movements become more important as other movements decrease in size.

The player's hands (*see* below) show the outcome of such technique.

Skilful players learn to throw with one or two hands. They adapt the power of a throw by increasing or decreasing the size of movements and the amount of body involvement. They prepare in ways that anticipate the direction as well as the force required for a pass. They control the direction of the flight of the ball by adjusting the point of release, by stepping to face the aiming point and by following through in that direction. They aim at a point in space where the receiver *will* arrive by the time the ball has travelled through the air.

◀ *Short pass technique*

One-handed pass: ▶
very high preparation

24

▲ *Player has thrown and will move to a space ready for her next contribution to play*

◄ *Concentrated assessment of where to throw before making a preparatory move*

▼ *Skilful players aim at a point in space where the receiver will arrive by the time the ball has travelled through the air*

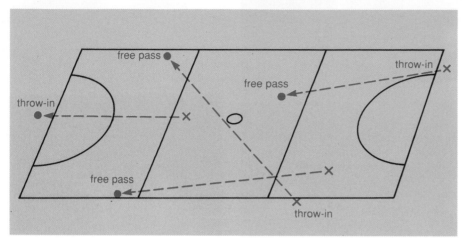

▲ *Fig. 11 Passing over a third: a free pass or throw-in is awarded at the point where the ball entered the incorrect third*

Details to complete *Rule 13*

Passing over a third: the ball must be caught or touched in the correct area. A free pass or throw-in is awarded at the point where the ball entered the incorrect third.

A player who lands with the first foot in the correct third is legal, no matter where the second foot lands. A player who lands on two feet simultaneously astride the line with the ball is penalised. This ruling applies at a throw-in.

For all faults in the Ball handling rule, a free pass is awarded to the opposing team except for the two faults noted, where a throw-in is awarded. The rule is applied at all times when a player is in possession of the ball, including at the taking of penalties.

Controlling skill – II

Once competitive play between opponents starts, the skills of *getting free* and *defending* are required. Like the primary skills, these two must combine good technique within the control required by the rules. The relevant rules are Obstruction (*16*) and Contact (*17*). Whether in attack or defence, both rules apply, though defenders are more in danger of breaking them (defaulting) because their aim is to 'stay close' whereas the aim of the attackers is to 'get away'. Umpires need careful observation to check who is at fault when players are close, for attackers may be equally at fault in a contest for space or for the ball. Much of the detail for both these rules is discussed in the context of 'Wise umpiring – part II' (*see* page 38). Here, the information highlights the relationship between rule and skill, and will include all the details which do not figure in the later section.

Obstruction *(Rule 16)*

Though obstruction is a fault, the rule identifies actions which *are* allowed as well as those which are not.

Skills for defending players:

● 'An attempt to intercept or defend the ball *may* be made by a defending player...'

The limitations set on this action concern the distance at which the defending player must be standing away from the player with the ball before attempting to defend. This distance is always measured on the ground; it is always a minimum of 0.9 m (3 ft); it is measured between one foot of the player with the ball and the nearer foot of the defending player. The *one foot* of the player with the ball is determined by that player's footwork when she receives the ball. It is:

(a) her landing, grounded or pivoting foot if it remains on the ground

(b) the spot on the ground where the landing, grounded or pivoting foot was if she subsequently lifts it

(c) the nearer foot to the defending

▲ *A player may attempt to intercept or defend the ball by jumping towards the player with the ball*

player if she lands on and remains grounded on two feet, but if she lands on two and lifts one, it is the foot still grounded which counts.

● 'From the correct distance, a defending player *may* attempt to intercept or defend the ball by jumping towards the player with the ball...'

The completion of this clause requires the umpire to make a judgement and the player to discipline the direction of the jump: '... but if the landing is within 0.9 m (3 ft) of that player and interferes with the throwing or shooting action, obstruction occurs'.

● 'A player *may* defend an opponent who has chosen to go, out of court...' (the skill) 'provided that the defending player does not leave the court or her own playing area in order to defend' (the limitation).

● 'A player *may* be within 0.9 m (3 ft) of an opponent without the ball,' and may attempt to prevent that opponent from trying to move to a free space on court or to move to catch a thrown ball, but all arm actions must be disciplined to prevent obstruction (*see* page 41).

• 'A player *may* be within 0.9 m of an opponent in possession of the ball, provided that no effort is made to defend . . .'

The skill here is to control movement and proximity because 'there must be no interference with the opponent's throwing or shooting action'.

Other defending actions *not* allowed:

• Even when at the correct distance from an opponent with the ball, a defending player may not *step* forward to lessen the distance.

At no time is the defending player penalised if the player in possession of the ball lessens the distance.

• The defending player may not prevent a player who is legitimately out of court from re-entering (*see* page 17).

• A player who is standing out of court may not attempt to defend a player who is on the court.

• Any action which 'intimidates' an opponent is illegal. It is for the umpire to decide when actions change from skilled effort to unpleasantness.

Attacking skill and obstruction:

• Attacking players can also be charged with intimidation, but otherwise obstruction can only apply to these players when they are not in possession of the ball. Their skills will include any of those described below. They are bound by the same ruling as any close-marking defence: 'when in close proximity, arm actions must be disciplined' (*see* page 41). However, no player is obstructing if the arms are outstretched to:

(a) catch, deflect or intercept a pass or feint pass

(b) obtain a rebound from an unsuccessful shot at goal

(c) signal momentarily for a pass, or to indicate the intended direction of movement.

All players should know what the obstruction rule allows and limits. Throughout, the rule presupposes that players understand: what are 'attacking and defending actions'; who is a 'defending player'; and the difference between 'intercepting or defending' the ball. The rule names some playing positions as 'attack' or 'defence', including WA and GA, WD and GD, though it is known that GS also is predominantly an attacking player while GK is a defender. In fact, all players are attackers if their team is in possession of the ball and defenders if they are in opposition. All players should practise attacking and defending actions within knowledge of the rule, even though some playing positions have a special focus on one or the other.

Attacking play

This is sometimes called 'getting free' or 'dodging'. It must be instigated with the economical arm movements required by the rule and involves:

• taking some positive action to get away from a close marking opponent. This may involve some sudden darting movements within a small space; running at full speed with the intention of outsprinting an opponent; body or step actions to achieve a sudden change of direction either during a run or to deceive an opponent before darting out

• constant adjustment of positions to 'hold space' in a chosen spot on court until team-mates are ready to respond to a 'momentary signal to indicate the intended direction of movement'. Shooters use such skill often, though other players may choose to adopt such action especially for a free pass or a throw-in

• observation of team-mates to assess who is in a good position to receive the next pass, either because they have clear space available or will be seen easily by the previous receiver. The observer will either move to receive that pass or to position for a subsequent pass

• catching the ball in a variety of ways

• assessing where to throw, choosing the best throw and executing a successful pass.

Players in possession of the ball in the photograph illustrate a number of these skills. The C is 'running at full speed' though in anticipation of the GS's passing problems ('observation of team-mates') rather than 'to get away from a close marking opponent'. The GA is positively 'holding space', although she has not positively signalled a movement or for a pass because she knows she is too near the circle edge to be in a good shooting position. She could easily 'dart' out to the free space forward and right of

her, but is unlikely to do this because neither shooter would be in the circle. The WA is also positively holding her position to keep open that very useful space to her right. She and her opponent appear to be in quite forceful contact and we cannot know which one instigated this. Judging by the stable balance of the WA compared with the more insecure stance of her opponent, it might be guessed that the WA has been

the more positive one. The GS is 'assessing where to throw'. She has problems because her opponent defending the ball is also obscuring her vision of the circle players. However, the anticipation of the C and the positioning of the WA, combined with the GA signalling through her *non*-activity ('Not me yet!'), suggest the attacking team will successfully retain possession. Note the red WA standing offside.

Defending play

Also called 'marking', defending play is always committed to stopping opponents receiving the ball in order to gain possession and start the counter-attack. Defenders are trying to intercept, which means catching or deflecting the ball intended for one of the attackers, or to defend the ball, which means taking action near the ball to make throwing or shooting difficult for the attackers and causing an inefficient pass (*see* photographs pp. 14–15).

This last action is the one which causes most obstruction faults by defending players. Umpires should watch that defenders: are not positioned closer than the correct distance; do not step forward in their attempt to take action; do not land from a jump and interfere; and do not intimidate the player rather than defend the ball.

Apart from this alternative focus on the ball, defenders should:

● in order to intercept a pass, concentrate on staying very close to opponents, trying to anticipate the timing of their intention to dodge

● concentrate on reading where an opponent wants to move and maintain close marking in conjunction with positioning in order to block the attacker's pathway to that space, but without using arm movements 'other than those involved in natural body balance'
● be active in spaces slightly away from opponents to tempt an unwise pass to what appears to be a 'free attacker', or to take options away from attackers who are trying to move positively to free space.

The last two skills are illustrated in the photograph above. The GK knows that the GS may try to move in a pathway parallel to the goal line towards the centre, but her attention and balance prove she is anticipating this. By staying slightly away from the GS she is 'tempting' her while taking away her option to dodge to the left. The attention of both the GD and the C is on the pathway of the running GA who will be hoping to enter the circle, though the GD may also switch easily to mark a throw from the red centre, either across the circle or to the GS. The black centre can easily check, using a push off her left leg to swerve towards the player who might receive the pass across the circle (this player's feet can just be seen).

Collectively, the three defenders have limited space and therefore the attacking players' options and their concentrated attention prove it has been intentional.

Contact *(Rule 17)*

Contact is a fault. Again, the name of the rule describes the fault, but unlike obstruction there are no instructions which define what a player *may* do and all restrictions apply equally to attackers and defenders. What is not allowed is discussed with illustrations on pp. 39–40.

The Official Rules refer to a number of actions to illustrate contact, using such words as 'push', 'bump', 'trip', 'knock', 'charge' and 'hold', but sum up all the restrictions in another clause:

> *A player shall not contact another on any other occasion or in any other way in such a manner as to interfere with the opponent's play.*

Umpires are also required to evaluate whether a player *causes* contact 'if taking up a position so near an opponent that contact cannot be avoided' or 'if moving so quickly into the path of a moving player that contact cannot be avoided'.

Contact with the ball is wrong and the defaulter may be the attacker who touches the defending player while trying to pass, or the defender while attempting to defend the ball. A defender who is at the legal distance but makes contact with the ball should be penalised. The intention of this rule is absolutely explicit. Contact in netball is not allowed, but it is acknowledged that some contact does not 'interfere with an opponent's play'. (The umpires' responsibility to assess is discussed in the next section.) The players' responsibility is confirmed here. All attacking and defending skills should be practised with a concern for physical control which will keep players safe.

Comparable physical control is required throughout the game. The Footwork and Ball handing rules combined with the Obstruction and Contact rules together define skills which need to be precise, economical and superbly disciplined. Since they are required by players operating in fairly restricted playing areas (*see* court dimensions with Offside and Out of court rules), the requirements are emphasised. For netball players the challenge and excitement is to work to become stronger and faster, versatile and daring, without losing control, balance and precision. The Contact rule sums up this challenge.

The penalty for breaking any aspect of the Obstruction and Contact rules is dealt with in the next section.

Netball's challenge is to be strong, fast, ▶ *versatile and daring, without losing control, balance and precision*

Controlling the game

Playing faults are penalised in different ways. This section develops knowledge of the rule which governs the taking of penalties (*Rule 18*); explains how the umpires act to administer those penalties and to control the game with the assistance of other match officials (*Rule 3*); and concludes with a variety of factors which concern match control but which are not related to playing faults (*Rules 5, 6 and 7*).

Conducting penalties (*Rule 18*)

The penalties awarded for the breaking of rules are:

- free pass
- penalty pass or penalty pass or shot
- throw-in
- toss-up.

Penalties for discipline problems are dealt with as a separate issue.

With the exception of the toss-up, penalties are awarded to a team, not to a player. A team may decide which player shall take the penalty, as long as that player is allowed in the area where the penalty is awarded. Because the team has the right to make this decision once a penalty is awarded to them, opposing players cannot prevent them taking the ball or moving to the place on the court where the umpire has indicated that the penalty should be taken.

Free pass

A free pass is awarded:

- when a single player is offside (*Rule 9*)
- when a single player moves into the centre third before the umpire's whistle at the start of play (*Rule 11*)
- for receiving a centre pass in the wrong area of the court (*Rule 12*)
- when a shooter attempts a shot after being in contact with the ground outside the goal circle (*Rule 15*)
- for all ball handling faults (*Rule 13*)
- for all footwork faults (*Rule 14*)

- if a late arrival enters the game without following the proper procedures (*Rule 5*)
- when a captain fails to report to the umpires and the opposing team captain that her team has changed playing positions or made a substitution during a stoppage for an interval or an injury (*Rule 6*)
- if an injured player subsequently returns to the vacant position in a game without following the proper procedures (*Rule 7*)
- if one player ready to be involved in a toss-up moves before the umpire's whistle (*Rule 18.4*).

Penalty pass

A penalty pass is awarded for all actions which contravene the Obstruction and Contact rules (*Rules 16 and 17*). If the award is given inside a goal circle the shooters are offered a penalty pass or a shot, in which case a shooter may choose which she takes and is not required to indicate her choice. This penalty is also awarded to the shooting team if a defence moves the goalpost in a way which interferes with a shot at goal.

There are similarities between a free pass and a penalty pass in that both involve a 'pass' taken by the non-offending team from that point where an offence occurred, but the penalty pass is awarded for misdemeanours which are considered to have a more adverse effect on the game and therefore the offending player has to stand beside and away from the thrower until the ball has left that player's hands. However, another player could defend the pass, as can happen with a free pass. Free passes are always taken where the offence occurred, but for a penalty pass an umpire may choose to indicate the spot where the non-offending player is standing if that player would be disadvantaged by taking the penalty where the offending player is standing.

For example, if a centre leans over the goal circle and makes contact with a shooter who has the ball in her hand, the fault is 'contact' (*Rule 17*). The offender is standing *outside* the circle, but as the interference could have disturbed a shot at goal, the umpire could decide to award a penalty pass or penalty shot inside the goal circle rather than a penalty pass outside. It is the

umpire's decision and she will have evaluated the possible advantage or disadvantage to the non-offending team in making her choice. When a penalty shot is offered as an alternative, the same restriction is placed on the offender, i.e. she must stand beside and away from the shooter until the ball is released (though the centre will not enter her offside area to do this in the example above).

▲ *When a penalty shot is offered as an alternative to a penalty pass, the offender must still stand beside and away from the shooter until the ball is released*

Should two offenders be involved in an incident, both must stand out until the ball is released. If defenders move too soon, the penalty is re-taken.

'Where the fault occurred' must be indicated by the umpire on all other occasions. For example, offside is a fault, so the free pass is taken in the offside area at the point where the offending player first crossed the boundary line. A

▼ *Umpire indicating where the fault occurred*

free pass for a footfault by the centre taking a centre pass is given inside the centre circle if she faulted while still in the circle, and outside if she had stepped out and then broken the rule. A shooter attempting a shot after stepping back outside the goal circle while holding the ball is penalised and the free pass is taken inside the circle where the shot was attempted, because the shot is the fault.

Throw-in

A throw-in is taken outside the court where the ball first crossed the line. When all players are on the court and the umpire has checked that the thrower is in position close to but not on the line, she will say 'play' to signal that the pass may be taken.

The throw-in is awarded for all out-of-court infringements (*Rule 10*) and for most of the faults which the team in possession might incur while taking a throw-in, when it is termed a penalty throw-in. It is given when the team in possession:

- fails to wait for the umpire to say 'Play'

- breaks the Footwork or Ball handling rules after 'Play' but before throwing the ball
- moves a foot on to the line or into court after 'Play' but before throwing the ball
- steps behind an offside area before releasing the ball.

Other faults which occur at a throw-in are when:

- the ball passes over a complete third of the court. The penalty is a free pass at the point where the ball entered the incorrect third
- obstruction or contact occurs involving a defending player on court. Either player might be at fault. The penalty pass (or penalty pass or shot) is awarded to the non-offending team and is taken on court.

If the thrown ball fails to enter the court a penalty throw-in is taken from the original point. If the thrown ball travels across the court area and passes out again elsewhere, a throw-in is awarded to the opponents at the new place.

Toss-up

A toss-up is action taken by the umpire between two opposing players. The players are positioned to give a distance of 0.9 m (3 ft) between the nearest foot of each. They may choose how to stand but must have their arms straight and hands at their sides. They must be facing their own attacking goal end, and they must remain still after the umpire has checked their positions until the whistle is blown.

A free pass is awarded if one player does move and it may be taken by any onside member of the opposing team, not necessarily the non-offending player in the toss-up.

The umpire has to ensure that she releases the ball mid-way between the two players, flicking it upwards not more than 60 cm (2 ft) in the air when the whistle is blown.

◄ *Umpire conducting a toss-up*

The ball rests on the palm of the umpire's hand in the correct ready position, just below the shoulder level of the shorter player's normal standing position. Prior to this, she will have confirmed the accuracy of their stance, moved forwards and, after a momentary pause, blown the whistle and simultaneously flicked the ball upwards.

The toss-up is awarded for all simultaneous offences by two opposing players, including:

- offside, with one or both having caught or made contact with the ball (*Rules 9 and 11*)
- action causing the ball to travel out of court (*Rule 10*)
- contact which interferes with play (*Rule 17*).

The toss-up is also taken to put the ball into play when:

- two opposing players simultaneously gain possession of the ball (*Rule 18*), even if one of these players lands out of court (*Rule 10*)
- after an accident if play stopped while the ball was on the ground or the umpire failed to note who was in possession of the ball at the moment play stopped (*Rule 7*)
- the umpire cannot determine who last touched a ball which goes out of court (*Rule 18*).

Whenever possible, it is required that the two players involved in the incident shall take part in the toss-up, either at the point where the incident occurred or as near as possible to that point on court and in an area common to both. How to deal with exceptions allowed when offside gives problems has been explained under the Offside rule (*see* page 17). Very rarely, an incident involving an accident may require such rapid and total attention from the umpires that the location of the ball at that moment is not noted. On such occasions an umpire will re-start the game with a toss-up in what she judges to be the most appropriate area between appropriate opponents according to the state of play when the game stopped. If simultaneous actions cause the ball to go out of court over the line of an area not common to both players, the toss-up is taken on the court near the point where the ball went out between any two opposing players allowed in that area.

Advantage

Rule 18 gives umpires two responsibilities with regard to 'advantage'. Both require umpires to exercise judgment, though the first, which has already been mentioned, is probably an easier decision than is the second. The first concerns the instruction that penalties are to be taken where an infringement occurs, though for a penalty pass or penalty shot 'the penalty shall be taken from where the infringer was standing except where this places the non-offending team at a disadvantage, when the penalty shall be taken where the obstructed or contacted player was standing'.

The outcome for the second ruling is more drastic. The umpire 'shall *refrain from blowing the whistle* to penalise an infringement when by so doing the non-offending team would be placed at a disadvantage'. On the positive side, this gives an umpire the right to ignore faults and to let a game flow without excessive interruption – players like this, and spectators do, too. On the negative side, a game may become uncontrolled if the umpire unwisely allows too many faults to pass unchecked or, worse, if the players feel they can take advantage of an umpire's apparent non-involvement.

The most commonly applied advantage in the first stages relates to offside decisions, particularly where a single offside player does not have the ball. It may be that the non-offending team is already in possession in a good position on the court and does not want to take the free pass elsewhere. In fig.12 a free pass should be awarded where the WA is standing, but advantage is played. Later, many obstruction incidents can be left unpenalised by the umpire, although she will signal advantage. If the speed of an attacking player's landing and subsequent pass are in no way interrupted by a close-marking opponent who has no time to move away to the required 0.9 m (3 ft), or a shot at goal is successful in spite of the defence stepping in towards the shooter, it is unnecessary to stop the game, and may positively disadvantage the attacking team to have a successful pass or shot ignored in order to take a penalty.

Only experienced umpires will be playing advantage in more debatable and subtle situations in addition to the fairly obvious and uncontroversial ones similar to those illustrated here.

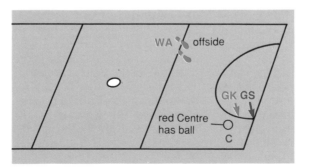

◀ *Fig.12 Playing advantage*

Umpires and other officials (*Rule 3*)

'There shall be two umpires who shall have control of the game and give decisions.' Control of the game is exclusively in their hands, though they should have the assistance of scorers and timekeepers. Umpires are bound by rules which define the extent of their responsibilities (*'They shall umpire according to the rules.'*) Many of these rules and responsibilities have already been mentioned. Umpires check that the conditions for play conform to the rules and in so doing examine equipment and players. They start and stop a game, acknowledge successful goals and generally control the organisation of the game. When they see playing faults, they blow the whistle and administer the appropriate penalty, and in order to do these things they are morally bound to have a thorough working knowledge of the rules.

The rules do not include words such as 'moral responsibility', but good umpires accept this interpretation of their responsibility to be objective and fair. The rules do say *'the decisions of the umpire shall be final and given without appeal'*, which illustrates that umpires wield considerable power. They should appreciate that their 'rights' must be regarded as 'responsibilities' and that their decisions sometimes require wisdom as well as accuracy. Responsibilities of this type are as follows.

Wise umpiring – part I

(1)   Umpires shall:

● decide on any matter not covered by the rules (*Rule 3.1.1*)
● not criticise or coach any team while a match is in progress (*Rule 3.1.5*)

(2)   During an interval either captain may appeal to the umpires for extra time to deal with emergencies (*Rule 3.4.3*)
(3)   Play may be stopped for injury or illness or any other cause. The decision to stop play shall be at the discretion of the umpire (*Rule 7.1*)
(4)   The breaking of the rules and/or the employment of any action not covered by the wording of the rules, in a manner contrary to the spirit of the game, is not permitted (*Rule 19.1*); the umpire shall penalise the infringement, by awarding a free pass, penalty pass or penalty shot, or a throw-in as appropriate to the situation (penalty for *Rule 19.1*).

Wise umpiring – part II

Responsibilities of a different type are implied by some rules which give specific instructions to umpires while adding a phrase which requires an umpire to evaluate players' intentions, actions or outcomes.

The advantage clause certainly comes into this category. The rule gives a specific instruction: *'umpires shall refrain from blowing the whistle ...'*, but only when evaluation has led to a judgement that *'by so doing the non-offending team would be placed at a disadvantage'*. *Rule 3* continues with the instruction, *'An umpire may call "advantage" to indicate an infringement has been observed and not penalised.'* The emphasis on 'may' is intentional, underlining yet again an umpire's right to choose and, therefore, her responsibility to judge. She may wish to keep all players alert to her involvement, she may wish to check

In this third instance (*left*) we do not know whether the players are touching. Unlike the photographer, the umpire would have moved to a position where she could see whether the players are in contact before presuming to judge whether it has interfered with play.

'Interfering with play' can be physically very obvious, causing players to lose balance, to lose possession of the ball or to register discomfort. More often the contact may be obvious to *see*, but less obvious to *evaluate*, especially if the contacted player catches and retains possession of the ball. It is the responsibility of an umpire to evaluate each situation as the outcome of previous actions, through the picture at the moment of contact to the probable result for the contacted player.

Rule 16 – Obstruction – provides the third example of this type of problem for the umpire.

◀ *Touching according to the camera, but . . .*

Contact! ▶

individual player's awareness of a playing fault, she may wish to be as unobtrusive as possible.

The intention alters either the manner and volume of the 'advantage' call or whether it is used at all. This part of the rule concludes with a specific instruction. *'Having blown the whistle for an infringement the penalty must be taken unless a goal is scored which is to the advantage of the non-offending team.'*

Another critical example of this type of wording is in *Rule 17.1* – Personal contact. *'No player shall come into personal contact with an opponent in such a manner as to interfere with play.'* Since umpires are obliged to *'umpire according to the rules'*, they are obliged to note all contact between opposing players and instantaneously decide whether the contact *interferes with play*. Observation, evaluation, reaction, happen in a sequence which is as fast as the action of a camera shutter. In the first photograph (*below left*) it is almost certain that the defending player initiated the contact, since the catcher has jumped up straight, whereas the defender is coming in at an angle.

In the next case (*below right*) it is not certain which player caused the contact or whether the catcher is disturbed by it. An umpire would have observed the action prior to this camera shot in order to judge the outcome depicted. Note also the foot contact in the circle.

Obstruction of a player
not in possession of the ball

A player is obstructing if, within a distance of 0.9 m (3 ft) measured on the ground from an opponent without the ball, any movements are employed by that player, whether attacking or defending, which takes the arms away from the body, other than those involved in natural body balance.

In the current context, the umpire has positive instructions to note that '*the player is obstructing if ... the arms are taken away from the body*'. However, evaluation is required to judge whether the arm movements are '*those involved in natural body balance*'. Arm actions which assist balance, changes of direction and running and jumping are 'natural', but it is for the umpire to judge when they change to become positive and intentional barriers.

Rule 16 provides three more examples where specific instructions to penalise for obstruction are implemented only if the umpire *interprets* the action as obstruction according to the rule.

▲ *Arm action*

41

16.2   From the correct distance, a defending player may *attempt to intercept or defend the ball by jumping forwards towards the ball, but if the landing is within 0.9 m (3 ft) of that player* and interferes with the throwing or shooting motion, *obstruction occurs.*

16.3   A player may *be within 0.9 m (3 ft) of an opponent in possession of the ball providing no effort is made to defend* and there is no interference with that opponent's throwing or shooting action.

16.6   When a player with or without the ball intimidates *an opponent it is obstruction.*

In spite of these examples of more difficult umpiring procedures, most instructions for umpires are precise and specific. These instructions are now grouped into four categories with the rule references listed.

▼ *Fig. 13 An umpire's area of control*

Area of control
3.1.5 (i), (ii), (iv)

Other aspects of control
3.2.1 (ii), (iv)
3.2.2

Procedures
3.1.2
3.1.3
3.1.5 (iii), (x), (xi)
7

Advice
3.1.4
3.1.5 (v), (vi), (vii)

Area of control

Fig.13 shows the area and lines controlled by one umpire. She is responsible for all decisions in this area throughout the game. She may not interfere in the other half of the court, though she should remain attentive in case the other umpire appeals to her for an opinion. For this side line and goal line she will deal with all out of court decisions, administer the resulting throw-in, attending also to any infringements

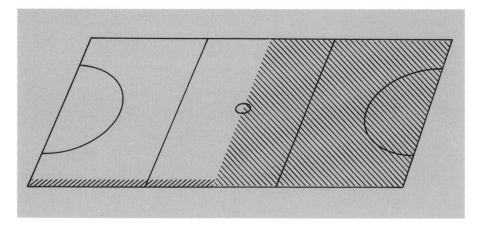

on court which affect the throw-in. She also deals with faults involving players who have left the court voluntarily over either of these two lines.

Other aspects of control

These relate to the umpire's relationship with the scorers and timekeepers. She should:

● signal to the scorers when a goal is scored, taking particular care to signal a disallowed goal. If no scorers are on duty, both umpires should keep their own score during the game
● keep a personal record of who is due to take a centre pass and signal this by raising an arm sideways towards the goal end of that team as soon as possible after a goal is scored. If the other umpire or the scorers disagree with the signal, take time to discuss it together. making reference to the score sheet to determine the correct team
● signal all stoppages and re-starts to the timekeeper: respond to the timekeeper to signal an interval or end of game.

Procedures

Procedures start before the game with the checking of the court, equipment and players. When the players are in position on court, the umpires toss to determine which half of the court each controls. The umpire who wins the toss is required to take the end previously designated the northern end. Thereafter, play *starts* in response to an umpire's whistle:

● at the beginning of the game, by the umpire into whose goal circle the team with the first centre pass is aiming
● after a goal is scored, by the umpire in whose half the goal was scored
● after an interval, by the umpire into whose goal circle the team re-starting play is aiming
● after a stoppage for which time has been taken, play resumes after the designated time, on the umpire's whistle.

Play *stops* in response to an umpire's whistle:

● when a playing fault is observed. The umpire deals with the penalty and play re-starts without a signal except that the umpire will say 'Play' for a throw-in to be taken, or will take a toss-up
● in response to an umpire's observation of an accident or her acknowledgement of an appeal to deal with an emergency. On these occasions, after blowing the whistle the umpire will instruct the timekeeper to take time
● at the end of the game in response to the timekeeper's signal.

Group A

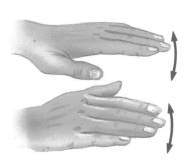

personal contact

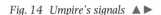

stepping

obstruction

Fig. 14 Umpire's signals ▲ ▶

After *stopping* the game *for a playing fault*, the umpire should state the infringement (e.g. Footwork) and penalty (Free pass to the red team) while signalling to clarify the information. These signals either give information about the fault (Group A) or about some aspect of control (Group B).

held ball

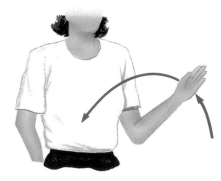

offside/breaking/over third

take time

direction of pass

toss-up

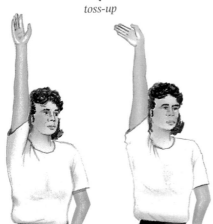

goal scored   *advantage*

Procedures affecting the control of *stoppages* include the following; the umpire should:

● instruct the timekeeper to take time whenever it is necessary to stop play because of injury, illness or some other emergency. Expect notification from the timekeeper when the two minutes allowed to decide whether the injured player is fit to continue have passed. Inform her of what time is being allowed for other emergencies; this time should always be as short as possible

● during such a stoppage, check that all other players remain on the court and that they do not receive coaching from any non-playing official
● to resume after the stoppage, re-start at that point where the ball was when play stopped, signal to the timekeeper and blow the whistle. Normally, therefore, re-start with a pass, a shot or an appropriate penalty. If the ball was out of court, re-start with a throw-in. If possession of the ball and/or the position on court is uncertain, re-start with a toss-up.

Advice

Advice which is set out in *Rule 3* is as follows; the umpires should:

- ensure that the colour of their clothing is distinct from that of the players: white or cream is ideal. Non-slip shoes suitable for fast movement should be worn
- move to keep in the best place to see play. Include movement along the whole of the goal line, a substantial part of the side line and even on to the court if necessary, though normally this should seldom occur. If the ball hits an umpire who is on court she should assess whether players have been disadvantaged. If they have, give a free pass to that team; if not, play continues
- when a toss-up is awarded on the far side of the court, an umpire may choose to appeal to the other umpire to take the toss.

Team officials

Team officials are (*Rule 3* cont.): coach, manager, captain, physiotherapist or doctor, or other registered medical person.

The captains shall (*Rule 3.4*):

- notify the umpires and opposing captain if substitutions and/or team changes are made
- appeal to the umpires for extra time during an interval to deal with an emergency
- have the right to approach an umpire during an interval or after the game for clarification of any rule.

Team officials shall (*Rules 2, 6, 7*):

- agree with other team's officials the duration of play when the full hour is not used
- notify the scorers of any substitutions or team changes made during play
- decide whether an injured player is fit to continue at the end of the two minutes allowed for such a stoppage.

Team officials shall *not*, during a game, direct play from off the court (*Rule 20*).

Rules 5, 6, 7

Other matters which concern the control of the game rather than the skill of playing are set out in Late arrivals (*Rule 5*), Substitution and team changes (*Rule 6*) and Stoppages (*Rule 7*). In these rules,

some procedures are similar and for this reason, the three are grouped at this point.

A *late arrival* is allowed to join a game which started without her team using a replacement. for her. Controlling her entry is identical with that required for an *injured player* who was left off court when play resumed after a stoppage, and no substitute was used. Both may play if there is a vacant position on court but neither may enter the game while play is in progress.

After notifying the umpires, they may take the court:

- after a goal has been scored, but only in the vacant position
- immediately following an interval or at a stoppage for injury or illness. In these cases, team changes may be organised.

In both cases, if a substitute had played in the vacant position, the late arrival/injured player may not enter the court except as a normal substitute bound by the rulings for substitution.

The *penalty* if either enters the court illegally is a free pass to the opposing team where the ball was when play was stopped. The player concerned shall leave the court until the next goal is scored or until after the next interval (whichever comes first).

Up to three *substitutions* are allowed during play. A player is called a 'substitute' (also a 'reserve'); replacing a player is called 'making a substitution'. Therefore, a team may have three substitutes and, by choice or due to injuries, use all three to make three substitutions. A team may bring one, make a substitution and subsequently make a second substitution or even a third, by returning substituted players to the game at later stages.

Penalty: should a team illegally attempt to make more substitutions, that player must leave the court, may not be replaced and no team changes are permitted unless the player is the centre, in which case her team may move just one player to act as centre.

The rule governing a *stoppage* for injury, illness or any other situation accepted by the umpires as an emergency, has been referred to previously.

An interval (half-time, etc.) may also be considered a stoppage in the present context.

● Substitutions may be made during a stoppage.
● Both teams may substitute during a stoppage if they wish.
● Substitutions must be notified to the other team, umpires and scorers (*see* 'Team officials') and failure to do so is penalised by awarding a free pass to the opposing team as soon as the umpire notices the substitution on court: the free pass is taken where the ball was when play was stopped; and after time has been allowed for the captain of the other team to substitute and/or make team changes if desired. However, the defaulting player is allowed to remain in play.

Team changes are also permitted during stoppages when players on court may rearrange their playing positions. Such changes may or may not involve using a substitute at the same time.

Team changes must also be notified. Failure to do so incurs the same penalty as failure to notify substitutions.

Discipline *(Rule 19)*

The previously quoted sections from *Rule 19* on page 38 sum up the attitudes required of players and the powers of an umpire in response to poor discipline. Rule-governed behaviour and good spirit are expected throughout the game, including stoppages and 'dead ball' situations. Umpires apply a penalty *as appropriate to the situation* against defaulting players, but may also send a player off the court *for rough or dangerous play or misconduct.*

Normally, the first procedure is to warn the player. Thereafter, the defaulting player may be sent off for a period deemed appropriate by the umpire. That player may not be replaced, though if she is a centre, her team may move one player to act as centre. After the suspension period the defaulting player may return as a goal is scored. She must return to her original place, as must the temporary centre.

For *Rule 20* Discipline of others refer to page 46. An umpire should warn any defaulting official and, therefore, may penalise the team which it is felt may benefit from the official's actions.

Index

This index is divided into two parts: the first is structured by the ordering of the game's rules in the Official Rules book (so that the two publications may be used in conjunction with one another); the second part deals with the game's skills and techniques.